The Life of
Harriet Tubman

Emma Lynch

www.heinemann.co.uk/library

Visit our website to find out more information about **Heinemann Library** books.

To order:
 Phone 44 (0) 1865 888066
 Send a fax to 44 (0) 1865 314091
 Visit the Heinemann Bookshop at www.heinemann.co.uk/library to browse our catalogue and order online.

First published in Great Britain by Heinemann Library, Halley Court, Jordan Hill, Oxford OX2 8EJ, part of Harcourt Education.
Heinemann is a registered trademark of Harcourt Education Ltd.

Editorial: Lucy Thunder and Harriet Milles
Design: Richard Parker and
    Tinstar Design Ltd (www.tinstar.co.uk)
Picture Research: Melissa Allison and Fiona Orbell
Production: Camilla Smith

Originated by Repro Multi-Warna
Printed and bound in China by
    South China Printing Company

The paper used to print this book comes from sustainable resources.

ISBN 0 431 18094 6
09 08 07 06 05
10 9 8 7 6 5 4 3 2 1

British Library Cataloguing in Publication Data
Emma Lynch
Harriet Tubman. – (The Life of)
973.7'115'092
A full catalogue record for this book is available from the British Library.

Acknowledgements
The Publishers would like to thank the following for permission to reproduce photographs:
pp. **4**, **19** Corbis; p. **6** Mary Evans Picture Library; pp. **7**, **13**, **17**, **18**, **23** Getty Images/Hulton Archive; pp. **8**, **9**, **15** Sean Victory/Harcourt Education Ltd.; p. **10** Illustrated London News; p. **11** Lee Snider/Corbis; pp. **12**, **14**, **16**, **25** Library of Congress; p. **20** Chris Honeywell; p. **21** Soul of America; p. **22** Corbis/Bettmann; p. **26** Collections of the National Underground Railroad Freedom Center; p. **27** Getty Images

Cover photograph of Harriet Tubman, reproduced with permission of Soul of America. Page icons: Hemera PhotoObjects.

The Publishers would like to thank Rebecca Vickers for her assistance in the preparation of this book.

Every effort has been made to contact copyright holders of any material reproduced in this book. Any omissions will be rectified in subsequent printings if notice is given to the Publishers.

Disclaimer
All the Internet addresses (URLs) given in this book were valid at the time of going to press. However, due to the dynamic nature of the Internet, some addresses may have changed, or sites may have changed or ceased to exist since publication. While the author and Publishers regret any inconvenience this may cause readers, no responsibility for any such changes can be accepted by either the author or the Publishers.

Contents

Words shown in the text in bold, **like this**, are explained in the Glossary.

Who was Harriet Tubman?

Harriet Tubman was born a **slave**. She lived in the United States of America in the 1800s. She escaped from slavery. Then she helped other slaves to escape, too.

This photo of Harriet was taken in the 1860s.

Harriet became the most famous leader of the Underground Railroad. This **organization** helped slaves to escape to places where there was no slavery.

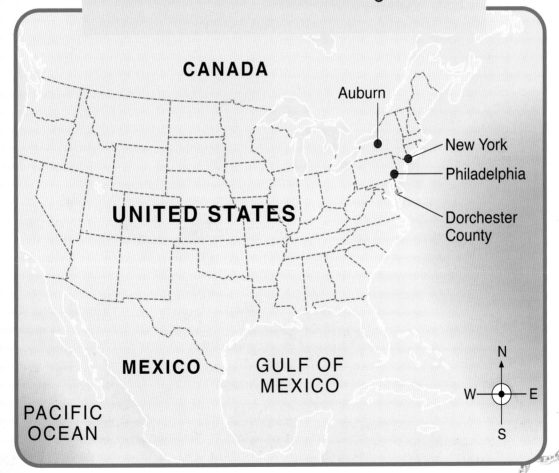

This map shows the places where Harriet lived or visited during her life.

CANADA

Auburn

New York

Philadelphia

UNITED STATES

Dorchester County

MEXICO

GULF OF MEXICO

PACIFIC OCEAN

N
W — E
S

Born a slave

Harriet was born around 1821 in Bucktown, Dorchester County in Maryland. Both of her parents were **slaves**. Harriet would be a slave too.

Harriet was born into a big family of slaves, like this one.

Slaves had to work all day in the fields.

At that time, many black people were slaves in the southern states of America. They worked on **plantations** owned by white people.

A slave's childhood

Harriet had a horrible childhood. She had to work in the fields for long hours every day. She never went to school. She was **whipped** even when she was small.

Harriet started work when she was only six years old.

When Harriet was about 12 years old, she was hit hard on the head by a white **overseer**. She would not help him to punish a **slave** who had tried to escape.

After she was hit, Harriet had **blackouts** all through her life.

Marriage and escape

In 1844, Harriet married John Tubman. In about 1849, she decided to escape from the **plantation**. John Tubman did not want to go with Harriet, or help her.

Slaves were often sold to other plantations. Harriet was scared that she might be sold, too.

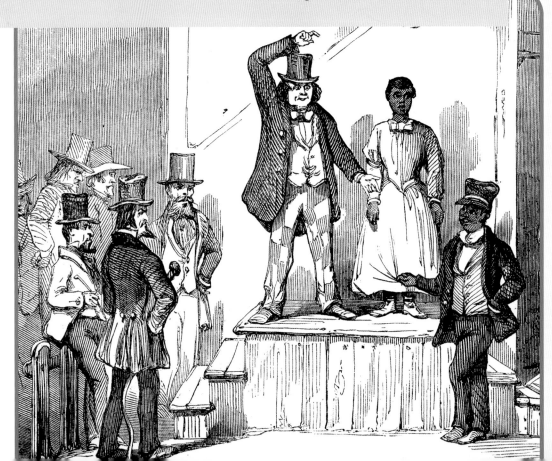

This **plaque** is now on one of the safe houses that was used to help slaves escape.

The GOODWIN SISTER'S HOUSE
ELIZABETH & ABIGAIL
UNDERGROUND RAILWAY
1821

A white neighbour helped Harriet. The neighbour told Harriet how to find a 'safe house'. The people in this house would help Harriet to escape from slavery.

The Underground Railroad

Harriet arrived at the safe house. She was put on a **wagon** and covered with a sack. Then she was carefully taken north, along the Underground Railroad.

Harriet escaped in a wagon, like this one.

The Underground Railroad was not a real railway. It was a secret **network** of safe houses, tunnels and roads. It was run by people who wanted to help **slaves** to escape.

Harriet was taken to Philadelphia, Pennsylvania. She found work there, as a housemaid.

Working for the Railroad

Harriet decided that she wanted to work for the Underground Railroad. First she helped her sister and her sister's children to escape to Canada.

Many white people did not agree with **slavery**. They helped the slaves to escape.

Chas T. Webb.   The Underground Railroad

Harriet was often in great danger when she went south.

Over the next 10 years, Harriet helped about 300 slaves to escape. In 1857 she brought her parents to Auburn, New York. It became their new home.

Wanted!

Sometimes the **slaves** got scared. Then Harriet would pull out a gun! She could not let them leave, in case they told people about the Underground Railroad.

People were offered a lot of money to catch Harriet and other escaped slaves.

$100 REWARD!

RANAWAY

From the undersigned, living on Current River, about twelve miles above Doniphan, in Ripley County, Mo., on 2nd of March, 1860, **A NEGRO MAN,** about 30 years old, weighs about 160 pounds; high forehead, with a scar on it; had on brown pants and coat very much worn, and an old black wool hat; shoes size No. 11.

The above reward will be given to any person who may apprehend this said negro out of the State ; and fifty dollars if apprehended in this State outside of Ripley county, or $25 if taken in Ripley county.

APOS TUCKER.

In the late 1850s, Harriet began to talk at anti-slavery meetings, like this one.

Harriet's secret trips were very dangerous, but she said that she 'never lost a passenger' on her railroad. She became famous for her work.

War work

In 1861, the **American Civil War** started. Harriet worked for the northern states. In South Carolina, she helped with a **raid** in which 756 **slaves** escaped.

Harriet worked as a nurse, a soldier, and a spy in the Civil War.

While Harriet was a nurse in the war, many soldiers were sick with **dysentery**. Harriet made a **remedy** from roots and herbs. It helped them to get better.

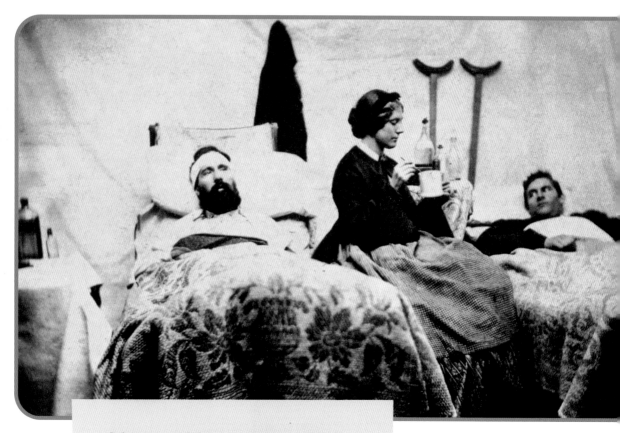

Many soldiers in the Civil War died from dysentery.

After the war

In 1863, **slavery** was **abolished** in the United States. The **Civil War** ended two years later. John Tubman died in 1867.

Harriet Tubman
THE MOSES OF HER PEOPLE

by Sarah Bradford

Introduction by Butler A. Jones

THE CITADEL PRESS
Secaucus, New Jersey

HARRIET TUBMAN.

A book about Harriet's life was published in 1869.

In 1869, Harriet married a soldier called Nelson Davis. Harriet was given many awards and medals for her work, but she was always poor.

In 1990, U.S. President George Bush made a special day to remember Harriet.

Harriet Tubman Day, 1990

By the President of the United States of America

A Proclamation

In celebrating Harriet Tubman's life, we remember her commitment to freedom and rededicate ourselves to the timeless principles she struggled to uphold. Her story is one of extraordinary courage and effectiveness in the movement to abolish slavery and to advance the noble ideas enshrined in our Nation's Declaration of Independence: "We hold these truths to be self-evident, that all men are created equal, that they are endowed by their Creator with certain unalienable Rights, that among these are Life, Liberty, and the pursuit of Happiness." ...

... In recognition of Harriet Tubman's special place in the hearts of all who cherish freedom, the Congress has passed Senate Joint Resolution 257 in observance of Harriet Tubman Day, March 10, 1990, the 77th anniversary of her death.

NOW THEREFORE, I, GEORGE BUSH, President of the United States of America, do hereby proclaim March 10, 1990, as Harriet Tubman Day, and I call upon the people of the United States to observe this day with appropriate ceremonies and activities.

Harriet's last work

Harriet went back to live in Auburn. She still wanted to help people. She worked to help women. She also set up a home for poor and elderly black people in 1908.

Harriet is standing on the left, with some of the **slaves** she helped to escape.

The home became known as the Harriet Tubman Home. Harriet Tubman died in 1913. Nobody knew her real age, but she was thought to be about 93 years old.

This is Harriet when she was a very old woman.

Why is Harriet famous?

We remember Harriet because she was so brave and strong. She helped hundreds of people to escape from **slavery**, even though it put her in great danger.

The **plaque** on Harriet's old house reminds people about her life.

"In memory of Harriet Tubman, called the Moses of her people. With rare courage she led over 500 black people up from slavery to freedom and rendered invaluable service as nurse and spy in the war. She braved every danger and overcame every obstacle. Withal she possessed extraordinary foresight and judgement so that she truthfully said – 'On my Underground Railroad I never ran my train off the track and I never lost a passenger'".

This picture of Harriet Tubman is called 'Moses'.

Harriet was called 'Moses' by the people she helped. In the Bible story, Moses led people to freedom. Harriet is an important person in American history.

More about Harriet

We can visit **museums** to find out more about Harriet. The Harriet Tubman Home in New York has letters, pictures and photos of Harriet's later life.

You can visit the National Underground Railroad Freedom Center in Cincinnati, Ohio, to learn more about slavery.

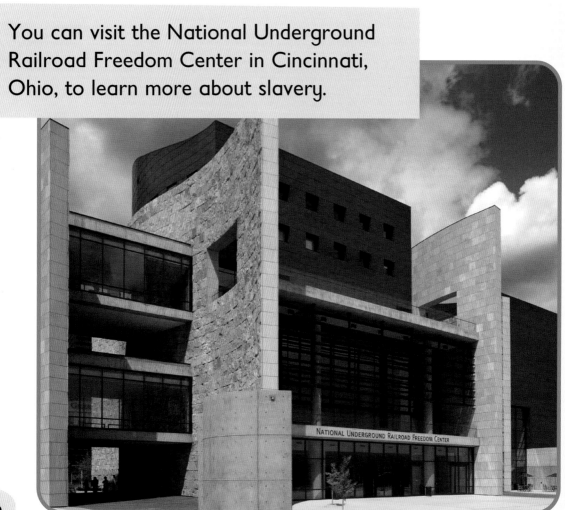

There are books and websites about Harriet Tubman's life. Some museums also have **artefacts** about **slavery**. These tell us how hard life was for slaves.

The United States **Government** made special stamps to remember heroes of the **Civil War**. Can you see Harriet's stamp?

Fact file

- Harriet's parents were Harriet and Benjamin Ross. They had 11 children who were all born into **slavery**.

- When Harriet was born, she was called Araminta Ross. When she got married, she decided to change her name to Harriet, which was her mother's name.

- When Harriet was a child, the northern and southern states of America were very different. There was slavery in the south, but people in the north did not agree with slavery. This started the **American Civil War**.

- Every year, people go to the Harriet Tubman Home on **Memorial** Day weekend. They celebrate Harriet's life.

Timeline

About 1821 Harriet is born

1844 Harriet marries John Tubman

1849 Harriet escapes to freedom

1850 Harriet joins the Underground Railroad

1851 Harriet brings her sister and her sister's children north

1857 Harriet brings her parents north

1861 The **American Civil War** starts

1865 The American Civil War ends

1867 John Tubman dies

1869 The first book about Harriet's life is published

1869 Harriet marries Nelson Davis

1908 Harriet opens the Harriet Tubman Home

1913 Harriet Tubman dies on 10 March

Glossary

abolish to get rid of something

American Civil War between 1861 and 1865 the northern states of America fought the southern states

artefacts things from long ago

blackout fall down and not remember what has happened

dysentery serious illness that is caught from bad food or dirty water

Government the people who run a country

memorial something to remind us of people who have died

museum place where pieces of art or parts of history are kept

network people, places or things that link together

organization group that gets things done

overseer someone who makes sure that work is being done

plantation houses and fields where crops are grown

plaque sign, usually to remember someone or something

raid sudden attack

remedy something that makes people better

slave person who is owned by someone, and made to work for them

wagon horse-drawn cart

whip to hit a person or animal with a long cord

Find out more

Books

The Underground Railroad: The Story of Harriet Tubman, Vicky Shipton (Oxford University Press, 2003)

Escape North! The Story of Harriet Tubman, Monica Kulling (Random House Books for Young Readers, 2000)

Websites

http://www.harriettubmanhome.org
Official website with links to information about Harriet Tubman

http://www.nyhistory.com/harriettubman/life.htm
Website about Harriet's life, escape and work for the Underground Railroad

Places to visit

The Harriet Tubman Home
180 South Street, Auburn, NY 13201, USA
Tel: 001 (315) 252-2081

Harriet Tubman's Birthplace
Green Briar Road, Cambridge, MD 21613, USA
Tel: 001 (410) 228-0401

Index

Titles in *The Life of* series include:

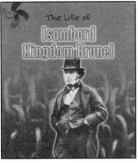

Hardback   0 431 18110 1

Hardback   0 431 18102 0

Hardback   0 431 18096 2

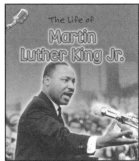

Hardback   0 431 18095 4

Hardback   0 431 18093 8

Hardback   0 431 18104 7

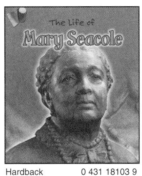

Hardback   0 431 18103 9

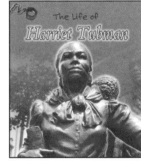

Hardback   0 431 18094 6

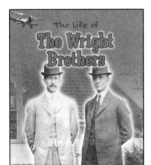

Hardback   0 431 18097 0

Find out about the other titles in the Heinemann Library on our website www.heinemann.co.uk/library